A DIE HARD Christmas

The Illustrated Holiday Classic

Written by Doogie Horner

Illustrated by JJ Harrison

INSIGHT
EDITIONS

San Rafael, California

'Twas the night before Christmas,
and up in the tower,
everyone was partying,
except one wallflower.

John McClane missed his wife; things just weren't the same since Holly had moved west and changed her last name.

H.M. GENNERO
DIRECTOR
CORPORATE
AFFAIRS

He tried to win her back, but still she said no, while, unbeknownst to them, there was trouble below.

A truck had pulled up,
and who should disembark,
but fourteen men
whose intentions were dark.

They spoke not a word and unloaded big crates.
They cut the phone lines and locked all the gates.

Karl swept the ground floor,
shooting every guard dead
while visions of bearer bonds
danced in his head.

John took off his shoes, making "fists with his toes."
It actually worked: "Well, what do you know!"

When out in the lobby there arose such a clatter,
he sprung to the door to see what was the matter.

When what to his wondering eyes should appear—
HOLY CRAP!
THERE ARE TERRORISTS HERE?!

John hid under a table where no one could see
and watched Hans question Mr. Takagi.
"I'm going to count to three; there will not be a four.
Give me the codes to open the vault door."

"I don't know the codes, so go ahead and shoot."
"Okay," said Hans Gruber, and ruined Takagi's suit.

John tried to call the cops
by pulling an alarm . . .

But instead called the bad guys,
who tried to cause him harm.

But John killed Tony, who had very small feet,
and sent him to the terrorists as a yuletide treat.

He put a Santa hat on the German, and, eyes all aglow,
wrote, "Now I have a machine gun, ho-ho-ho."

Karl was furious.
Tony was his brother.
He chased John across the roof,
and they shot at each other.

John was able to escape
through the ventilation shafts.
"Come out to the coast," he sighed.
"We'll have a few laughs."

At Nakatomi Tower,
Sergeant Powell appeared.
He checked the whole lobby
and saw nothing weird.

He was pulling away
but didn't get far
before Marco landed
on the hood of his car.

Powell drove away backwards, screaming in fright.
"Welcome to the party, pal!" John yelled with delight.

More police arrived, the FBI and a SWAT team.
But Hans didn't mind. It was all part of his scheme.

More rapid than eagles
his henchmen they came.
And he radioed and shouted
and called them by name.

Now Eddie, now James,
now Franco, now Uli!
On Fritz and on Karl—
hair long and unruly!

They shot the SWAT tank
with a surface-to-air missile
and knocked it away
like the down of a thistle.

Now John McClane
was angry indeed.
He blew up two terrorists
and called them "jerkweed."

Ellis told Hans, "Bubby, I'm your white knight!"
Hans shot him dead, giving the hostages a fright.

Hans went to go check
on the explosives' fuse
and saw that poor John
wasn't wearing any shoes.

John fled from Karl and Hans but alas!
He had to run barefoot over sharp, broken glass.

His feet, how they hurt.
His soles, oh so bloody!
John crawled to the bathroom
and called his good buddy.

John was weary and
ready to throw in the towel—
until he got a pep talk
from Sergeant Al Powell.

Powell was chubby and plump,
a right jolly old cop.
And he trusted the cowboy
in the tattered tank top.

But a reporter was probing
into McClane's life
and revealed that Holly
was actually John's wife!

Hans quickly flipped over
the gold picture frame.
"It's a pleasure to meet you . . .
Mrs. McClane."

His clothes all tarnished with ashes and soot,
John staggered to the roof, bloody and barefoot.

The explosives were wired to the rooftop with care in hopes that the hostages soon would be there.

John warned everyone the roof would soon blow as the chopper strafed him with high-powered ammo.

Around his waist he tied a fire hose tight.
And, screaming an oath, jumped into the night.

He dangled in the air and gritted his teeth,
while flames encircled the tower like a wreath.

Fiercely fighting his way back inside,
John yelled out, "Haaaaans!"
He was done trying to hide.

He limped to the vault like an old man on crutches
only to find Holly in his filthy clutches.

John dropped his gun,
put his hands on his head.
It seemed he and Holly soon would be dead.

But with a secret gun taped to his back,
John shot Hans in a surprise attack!

Hans fell out the window still holding Holly's arm
And slowly, deliberately, raised his firearm—

The tenacious villain
held on by his nails,
till John unhooked Holly's watch
and said, "Happy trails!"

Bearer bonds fluttered
like fresh fallen snow
as Holly embraced
her blood-spattered beau.

So Merry Christmas to all,
be kind to one another,
And, most of all,
yipee-ki-yay, motherfucker!

INSIGHT EDITIONS

PO Box 3088
San Rafael, CA 94912
www.insighteditions.com

Find us on Facebook: www.facebook.com/InsightEditions
Follow us on Twitter: @insighteditions

Library of Congress Cataloging-in-Publication Data available.

ISBN: 978-1-60887-976-2

Publisher: Raoul Goff
Associate Publisher: Vanessa Lopez
Art Director: Chrissy Kwasnik
Managing Editor: Alan Kaplan
Project Editor: Kelly Reed
Production Editor: Elaine Ou
Production Manager: Alix Nicholaeff

Illustrations by JJ Harrison

Insight Editions, in association with Roots of Peace, will plant two trees for each tree used in the
manufacturing of this book. Roots of Peace is an internationally renowned humanitarian organization
dedicated to eradicating land mines worldwide and converting war-torn lands into productive farms and
wildlife habitats. Roots of Peace will plant two million fruit and nut trees in Afghanistan and provide
farmers there with the skills and support necessary for sustainable land use.

Manufactured in China by Insight Editions